Stroodle the Labradoodle

TLS DeCoster

Stroodle the Labradoodle
Published by Meadowhawk Media LLC
Wilsonville, OR

Copyright © 2023 by TLS DeCoster All rights reserved.

No part of this book may be reproduced in any form or by any mechanical means, including information storage and retrieval systems without permission in writing from the publisher/author, except by a reviewer who may quote passages in a review.

All images, logos, quotes, and trademarks included in this book are subject to use according to trademark and copyright laws of the United States of America.

Publisher's Cataloging-in-Publication data

Names: DeCoster, T. L. S., author. | Jay, Heidi, illustrator.
Title: Stroodle the Labradoodle / written by TLS DeCoster; illustrated by Heidi Jay.
Description: Wilsonville, OR: Meadowhawk Media LLC, 2023. | Summary: When their family Labradoodle is about to give birth, Pippa finds herself left to her own devices to deliver the puppies.
Identifiers: ISBN 978-0-9892919-1-0
Subjects: LCSH Dogs--Juvenile fiction. | Friendship--Juvenile fiction. | Family--Juvenile fiction. | BISAC JUVENILE FICTION / Social Themes / Friendship
Classification: LCC PZ7.1 .D432 St 2023 | DDC [E]--dc23

Copyright owned by TLS DeCoster.
Illustrations by Heidi Jay copyright owned by TLS DeCoster.

QUANTITY PURCHASES: Schools, companies, professional groups, clubs, and other organizations may qualify for special terms when ordering quantities of this title. For information, email tls.decoster@gmail.com.

All rights reserved by TLS DeCoster and Meadowhawk Media LLC.
Printed in the United States of America.

For my lucky STARS~Jaden, Axel, Adeline & Victoria
Martina, Natalia, Jacob, & Vivi

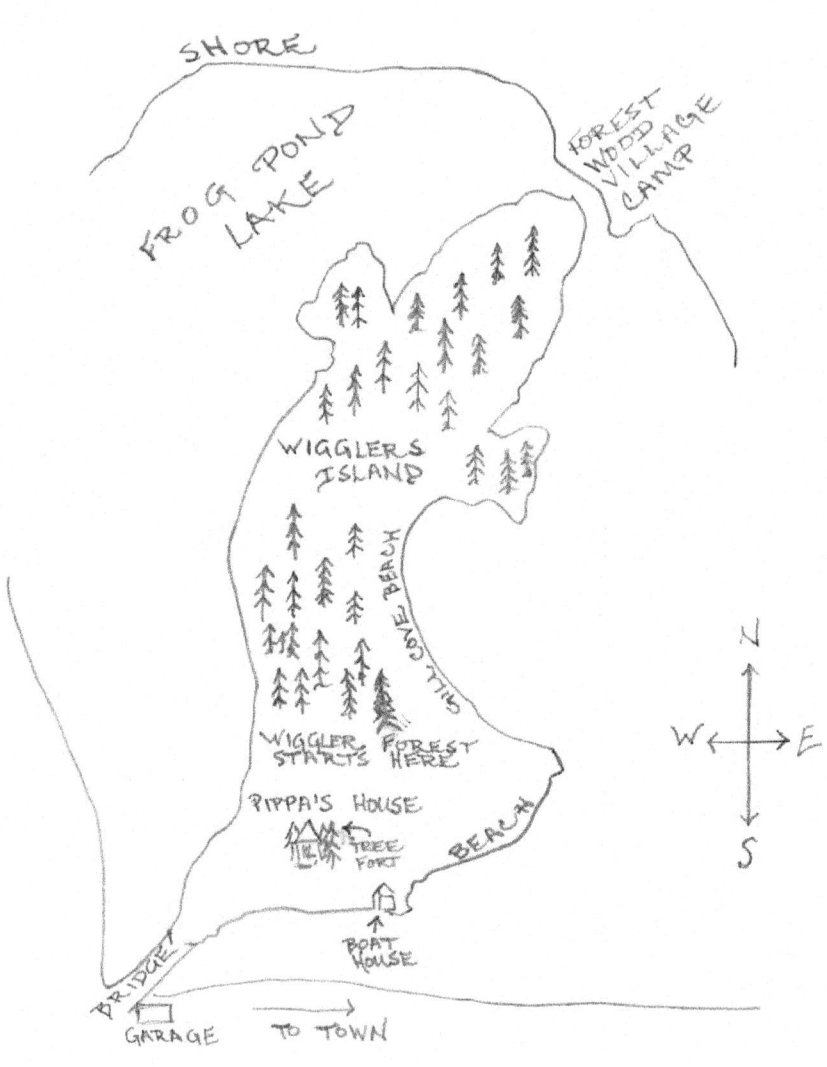

THE DOODLERS

Pippa Pinkerton: An adventurous child who is clever, empathetic, and outgoing. She loves growing up on Wigglers Island, where her father, grandfather, and great-grandfather grew up too. She enjoys swimming, dancing, playing the piano, and being outdoors—especially in her two-story treehouse. Pippa has long, dark brown hair that she wears in two braids and long dark eyelashes to match. She is half Hawaiian and looks forward to her visits to the Big Island of Hawaii.

Gia Lopez: Level-headed and always there for you, Gia is tall for her age and has dark brown, curly hair as thick as a horse's mane. She is top in her class in mathematics, known for putting stuff in order, and usually remains calm in stressful situations. She arrived in the US from Argentina at three years old with her mother after her father was killed in a horseback riding accident. Her mother married John Lopez a few years later, and he adopted Gia as his own daughter. Gia adores caring for the newborn foals and often declares that she loves everything about babies. They live on their ranch in Frog Pond, Oregon.

Britt Cline: The Baker of the Besties, Britt is half blind and doesn't allow anything to stop her from joining her friends for fun and frolic. She has dazzling blue eyes and medium blonde hair with bright blonde highlights that sits neatly on her shoulders. She usually has her guide dog, Bilberry, at her side. Britt's mother owns Cline's Café and Cupcakes, otherwise known as C3, where Britt spends many afternoons each week helping out and eating cupcakes with her friends. On occasion, she also visits the nearby university to test out new equipment and computer software for the blind or visually impaired.

Chapter One

Welcome to Wigglers Island

Pippa Pinkerton hopped up onto the front porch stairs of the old Frog Pond house. Her long, dark braids bounced from her front side to her back. She carried the mail under her arm and turned to admire the grapevines that rolled out over the nearby slopes of Oregon's Willamette Valley.

Pippa lived with her family on Wigglers Island in Frog Pond Lake. Named for the abundance of earthworms and frogs, the small island boasted one Victorian house with one modern family. Pippa loved the two-story boathouse with its spectacular views, fishing, and water sports. A private bridge connected the island to the mainland. No cars, but golf carts with unique colors transported people around the nearly eleven-acre haven.

A finger-like chestnut tree shaded Pippa's home. Rays of sunshine filtered through the leaves, casting shadows. A tire swing hung from a thick branch and a wooden spiral stairway wrapped around the trunk. The stairway led to a three-room, furnished treehouse that Pippa's grandfather built for Pippa's dad when he was a small boy. The Pinkertons have been living on Wigglers Island for generations.

One of the tree branches grew alongside the attic window, high up on the third floor of the Frog Pond house. A couple of years prior, Pippa's father, Professor Pinkerton, had built a small platform on the branch and connected a zipline from the attic to the treehouse. He rigged a safety harness outside of the window to prevent the children from falling while climbing in and out.

Pippa smiled and thought she was the luckiest girl in Frog Pond—and maybe the luckiest girl in the whole wide world! She went inside, and the screen door clapped shut behind her. She plopped the mail into an open-roof birdhouse on the counter marked MAIL. Suddenly, there was a dog bark—the sound Pippa's cell phone made when she got a text from her mom. Pippa reached into her pants pocket and saw one word:

Mom: Puppies? :-D

"Hmmm," Pippa said out loud. "Good question."

Peaches, the Pinkerton's apricot-colored Labradoodle, was due this week. *Where is everyone?* Pippa wondered.

"Hello?" she called from the kitchen. "Pops? Ryan?"

She walked down the hall to peek inside the den where Peaches was resting and waiting for her puppies.

"No puppies yet, Peaches? Isn't it about time? I'm tired of waiting."

Peaches looked up at Pippa with her face tilted to the side as if to say, *Yes, I'm tired of waiting too!* Pippa shot a one-word text message back:

Pippa: Nope :-(

Pippa left the door open and turned to check upstairs for the rest of her family. Out of the corner of her eye, she saw a flash of yellow polka dot bed sheets. A small figure was swinging down from the top of the banister and came flying across the entry hall. He crashed right into Pippa, smooshing them both into the door of the doggy delivery den.

"Ryan!" Pippa shouted as they both fell to the floor. "What do you think you're doing?"

Ryan hit his forehead on the corner of the door.

"Ouch!" he cried out. He held his hand over his eye. "You wrecked it! I'm Robin Hood, the Prince of Trees!"

"Do you mean Robin Hood, the Prince of *Thieves*?" Pippa corrected.

Blood began to trickle out through Ryan's fingers and down his face. Pippa's stomach turned. Ryan looked at his hand and screamed.

"I'm bleeding! Pippa! Pops! Pops!" He broke free from her arms and began to run through the house—first into the family room and then through the kitchen, the dining room, and onward to the living room, the library, and back to the entry hall. He was running in a big circle.

"Stop running, Ryan!" Pippa panted, chasing after him. "Stand still for a moment, so I can check your forehead."

Blood dripped from his head to the floor. She followed the drops of blood around the house trying to catch him.

"I'm bleeding! POPS! POPS!" Ryan continued to scream.

Then Pippa had an idea. She turned around and ran in the other direction toward the kitchen. Ryan ran right into her.

"Gotcha," she said, clutching him to her. Her little brother's head came up to her chest. "Now hold still."

She remembered the last time Ryan had hit his head, tripping on the back porch stairs while on a butterfly hunt. He had bled a lot then, and Pops had said that head injuries do that. Ryan had received a butterfly stitch—perfect for a butterfly hunter.

Now Pippa led Ryan to the back porch and first aid kit.

"Please don't play the Prince of Trees, I mean Thieves, anymore," she pleaded and patted her brother on the back. "I don't think the house can take much more of it."

Her voice trailed off as a man came in through the screen door with mud on his shoes and a basket full of grapes.

"Thank goodness, Pops," said Pippa. "I was just about to go find you."

Professor Pierce Pinkerton took one look at his five-year-old son.

"Oh brother," he said. He set down the grapes and clasped his hands together. "I only left you for a few minutes."

"I'll give you one hint," said Pippa. "He tied sheets together."

"Not the Prince of Trees!"

"Yep," said Pippa, rolling her eyes. "That's exactly what it is. And when's he gonna learn that it's the Prince of *Thieves*, not Trees?"

She groaned.

"*Uggh*," said Pops, playfully mimicking his daughter. He winked at her and then knelt down in front of his son who was looking at him wide-eyed, breathing heavily. "Thank you for helping calm your brother down, Pip. Ryan, I'm just happy you haven't started using arrows."

"Oh gosh—don't give him ideas!" said Pippa, half-serious, half-joking. "Pops, I think we have to start locking the linen closet."

"Do I need a butterfly stitch again?" Ryan asked, squirming out of Pippa's arms. "I wasn't trying to catch a butterfly."

Pops wiped the blood off Ryan's head with a wet paper towel from the kitchen. His fingers skimmed over the bump. He folded the paper towel into quarters and placed it in Ryan's hands.

"Hold this paper towel right here for a minute," said Pops, bringing Ryan's hands up to the wound. "I'll get some ice, and we can keep putting pressure on it."

"Okay," Ryan pouted. His lips started to tremble, and tears welled in his eyes.

Pops returned with an ice pack.

"Now, let me take a better look," said Pops. He lifted Ryan's hands away from his face and tried not to look surprised. The paper towel was soaked through with blood. The pressure didn't seem to be slowing down the bleeding.

"Okay," said Pops, turning to Pippa. "I'll get my keys and run him to the emergency room."

Ryan started to whimper.

"Hey, Prince Ryan," Pops said soothingly, looking into his son's teary eyes. "I know this is scary. I am here with you. Do you think you can be brave like Robin Hood? I promise you will be fine." He gently smoothed Ryan's hair.

Pippa grabbed her dad's cell phone and wallet from the desk in the entry hall and handed them to him.

"I'm going to check on Peaches," she said. "She's been in her den all day." She looked down at all the little red drops on the floor. "But first, I will clean up this trail of blood."

Pops turned to his daughter.

"Thanks so much, Pippa. Now, about Peaches. It's up to you. Take another look at Mom's YouTube video on puppy deliveries. It's listed as 'whelping.' The vet said Peaches is supposed to deliver this week, but you never know. Keep your phone nearby in case you need to call or text. Or you can always, well, . . . Google it." He smiled. Pippa nodded her head.

"I can do this," she said.

"Hugapalooza," Ryan mumbled to Pops. "Yes, Hugapalooza . . . thanks, Ryan . . . ," Pops replied. The Pinkertons used the code word, Hugapalooza, as a reminder not to forget anything important—phones, wallets, lunch, or whatever else—before leaving the house. "Let me think. Do I have everything? Wait, I'll need your insurance card from inside the desk drawer." He walked over to the desk and grabbed it. "Let's go!"

Pops scooped Ryan up and headed out to his grape-colored golf cart. Pippa waved goodbye and closed the front door. She turned to face the makeshift delivery den.

"Here I come, Peaches."

When Pippa peeked in, Peaches was resting with her eyes shut, but she looked up at the sound of the door opening.

"This is a first for both of us," Pippa told Peaches, scratching her fluffy head. "I wish Mom was here." She decided to watch the YouTube video right away and ran upstairs to her dad's office. Pippa's mom, Suzanne Pinkerton, was up in Seattle, Washington, teaching a behavior clinic for dogs and their owners. Her book, *Do Behave! A Step-by-Step Guide to Train Your Puppy While Your Puppy Trains YOU,* was on the bestseller list. Mrs. Pinkerton posted monthly YouTube videos on puppy training and newborn puppies, and she had many followers.

Pippa pulled up a video called *Safe Puppy Deliveries: Whelping 101*. After a few minutes, she started worrying. *What if there are complications? What if I can't help Peaches and her puppies by myself?* She took a deep breath and tried to put those thoughts out of her mind.

"I can do this," she said out loud. Pippa felt butterflies in her tummy, and they were not the ones you hunt.

Chapter Two

Yes, You Can!

Pippa was deep into the second YouTube video when the doorbell rang.

"Who can that be?" she said, jumping up. *And how did they get over the bridge without ringing the bell?* Pippa ran over to the banister.

"Who is it?" she called out.

"It's me, Britt," came a voice through the door. "Can I come in?"

Of course, it's Britt, thought Pippa, letting out a sigh of relief. *She has the passcode to open the bridge gate.*

"I'm upstairs!" Pippa said excitedly. "Come on in. The door is open. I'll be right down." She took her phone out and texted Pops:

Pippa: Watching Mom's YouTube on puppy births. I can do this :)

She returned to her father's office. Pops texted back quickly:

Pops: YES, YOU CAN :)

Brittany "Britt" Cline let herself inside. Slowly, she felt her way along the wall. Britt was blind in one eye and partially blind in the other.

"I wanted to see if Peaches had her puppies yet!" she called out loudly so that Pippa could hear from upstairs. "My mother made us some treats, too. They are chocolate, gluten-free cupcakes with a surprise on top. Also, a peach strudel for your dad."

She placed the treats on the entry hall table and waited for Pippa.

"YUMMY!" Pippa called back. "Cline's cupcakes are the best! AND Pops *loves* your mom's strudel."

Pippa and Britt had been friends since the first grade. Britt's dog, a Labradoodle named Bilberry, was the father of Peaches's puppies. Bilberry's deep red, wavy hair complemented Peaches's curly apricot swirls. Everyone who knew the two Doodles was awaiting the birth with great excitement, imagining what cute puppies they would have.

Pippa's mom had trained Bilberry to be Britt's guide dog. Even though Britt could partially see and wore glasses, Bilberry's job was to help Britt find her way around and warn her if there was any nearby danger. He was also the best companion and friend. Bilberry slept by Britt's bed each night. He now rested on the porch outside Pippa's house with a fresh bowl of water.

Britt heard Pippa walk up to the banister.

"Hi Pippa. How's it going?"

"Hey. Peaches is doing fine. I was just watching my mom's YouTube video on puppy birth because my dad had to rush Ryan to the emergency room."

Britt looked up toward Pippa, worried.

"Long story...," Pippa said breathlessly. "Head wound, may need stitches. BUT," she blurted out, "I can do this!"

"Yes, you can!" laughed Britt encouragingly. "Sounds like another Ryan adventure."

She found her way to the delivery den, brushing up against the hanging sheets. She smiled knowingly.

"If you *want* to call it an adventure," said Pippa, as she headed back to the office. "I think he is more mischievous for sure."

"Hey there, Peaches," said Britt, crouching down. "Bilberry is outside relaxing while we wait for your pups to arrive." She leaned closer. Peaches was breathing hard.

"Pippa!" Britt called urgently. Pippa couldn't get down the stairs fast enough. Britt was kneeling near Peaches, scratching her ears.

"Everything is going to be fine," Britt told Peaches. She laid her hand on Peaches's moving tummy. Peaches whimpered as if to say, *When is this going to be over?*

"She is quite uncomfortable and restless," said Britt.

"Wow, I didn't even notice that earlier," said Pippa. "I'm always amazed how much you can sense things like that."

"Thanks," whispered Britt. "It's only natural. You know how sensitive my hearing is."

"Oh yes, I do," whispered Pippa with a twinkle in her eye. "You can hear *anyone* from across the room. By the way, is your brother's hair finally dry yet?"

They both giggled. Britt's sharp ears had helped them out in the past. A few years prior, their families had rented a place together at the beach, and Britt had overheard her older brother telling his friend to try Pippa's Hawaiian shampoo. The boys used it all week without asking Pippa if it was okay, and they were wasting so much of it. So, on the second to last day there, Pippa and Britt secretly replaced the shampoo with corn oil.

The next day, after hours of swimming in the ocean and playing in the sand, everyone took their showers, and the boys couldn't understand why their hair wouldn't dry. Unfortunately, they all got in trouble: the boys for not asking to use the shampoo and the girls for pulling the prank.

"Now, down to business," said Britt. "My mother and I watched your mom's YouTube video too. Do you have her whelping box ready?"

"Yes," said Pippa. "I also have a basket with medical supplies, cloth strips, and gloves. I think we are as prepared as we can be."

"Someone's here," said Britt. "I just heard the bridge bell."

"I'll go look," said Pippa, walking toward the window. "Oh! It's the vet, Dr. Drew. He must be here to check on Peaches."

She pushed the button on the security video camera by the door and spoke through the intercom.

"Hello, Dr. Drew!"

"Hi Pippa. Your dad messaged me and asked if I could stop by to check on Peaches."

"Oh great," she answered. "I'll buzz you in."

Pippa pushed another button. The electronic gate on the bridge opened. A young girl appeared, running and jumping behind the vet, and together they got into one of the guest golf carts. The girl was Gia Lopez, Pippa's other bestie. Pippa and Britt ran out to meet them as the golf cart pulled up to the front door.

"Gia!" Pippa smiled, hugging her friend. "I'm so glad you're here too."

Everyone entered the house, and Pippa led the way to the delivery den.

"I just left the Lopez Ranch to check on their new foal, a colt," explained the vet. "That's when I got your dad's text."

"I decided to tag along," Gia beamed. "I *love* new babies! Foals or puppies or baby people—they're all adorable!"

"It's been a little nerve-racking," admitted Pippa, "so I'm glad to see you both. Britt and I are doing our best to make sure Peaches is comfortable."

"Why don't you girls take a break while I check her over?" said Dr. Drew. "I saw some delicious-looking cupcakes out there on the desk that are calling your name. Those puppy faces are so creative!"

"My mother made those!" said Britt.

"I love cupcakes," said Gia. "Especially cupcakes made by Britt's mom."

Pippa's stomach rumbled as the girls headed over to the desk.

"I could use a snack," she said. She peered into the box of cupcakes. "Ooo, I want the one with fluffy ears. I love marshmallow and cream cheese frosting."

"I'm in," agreed Britt. "I smelled them baking *aaaall* morning."

"And you didn't eat one?" gawked Gia. "I admire your self-control!"

"Well, maybe one," said Britt, laughing. "But it did take self-control not to eat the whole batch!"

They laughed. Pippa tapped Britt's arm and held out her own for Britt to hold onto. Britt was great at getting around in open spaces, but when it came to navigating around furniture, she usually appreciated a little help. Pippa picked up the tray and led Britt and Gia into the breakfast nook to enjoy the goodies.

"I'll keep one out for you, Dr. Drew!" Pippa called. "I heard you love chocolate."

"Chocolate is *my* favorite too," said Britt. "It was so fun helping my mom design each puppy face."

Britt's mom, Chloe, was the owner of Cline's Café and Cupcakes. The university students affectionately called it C3 for short. C3 was a top destination and meeting place in town. On the weekends, the line could be seen going around the block. Britt worked as a cashier on summer mornings. The university kept her supplied with all of the newest equipment for the visually impaired. Her smartphone and C3's iPad included Braille buttons—buttons she could read by feeling them—to make it easier to take orders and check out customers.

"The Clines are quite imaginative when it comes to cupcakes, that's for sure!" said Pippa, as she gobbled down her chocolate cake. The big, floppy ears were gooey marshmallow deliciousness. The eyes were mini chocolate chips. "I love how each cupcake has a different face. Your mom is so creative."

Gia was quietly nibbling at her lemon cupcake. Her face puckered.

"It's SO sour," she said. "I love it."

She wiped a bit of the frosting off her nose and licked her fingers. Dr. Drew came into the kitchen to give his report.

"Well," he said, clapping his hands together, "you girls look like you have everything under control. Peaches is asleep, and it's a good thing for her to rest before her puppies arrive. It looks like she may have them during the night or sometime tomorrow."

"Oh wow!" squealed Gia. "My timing was perfect. First, I was there for our new foal, and now your new puppies!"

"I can't believe it either," said Britt. "I have to text my mom and tell her. Oh! And I'll give Bilberry the news too!" She walked out to the porch to find him.

"I think we are ready," said a determined Pippa.

"That's the spirit, girls," said Dr. Drew. "Please tell your dad I'll stop by around 10 a.m. tomorrow on my way back to the Lopez Ranch." He picked up a cupcake with a napkin. "If you need me, just send a text."

He started to walk away.

"Oh! I almost forgot." He opened his bag and took out a big

handful of soft collars, each a different color. "I figured you will need these to identify the pups after they're born."

He handed them to Pippa.

"You can do this," he said.

"YES, I CAN," said Pippa boldly.

Dr. Drew picked up his vet bag and waved goodbye. "Good luck. See you tomorrow, and thanks for the cupcake!"

Pippa turned to her besties.

"Guess what," she clapped with excitement. "Text your parents. I am having a sleepover!"

Chapter Three

Lights Out!

Pippa checked the items again to make sure she had everything she needed for the puppy delivery. She peeked in on Peaches. She was resting. Pippa turned on a dim lamp in the corner and left the door open. The kitchen clock read 8:35 p.m. She walked out the back door to join Britt and Gia on the covered porch.

The girls had baked a pepperoni and artichoke pizza with extra cheese on defrosted gluten-free dough Britt's mom sent over. Britt's sensitive stomach did better with gluten-free baked goods, so out of loyalty, Pippa and Gia had jumped on board too. They figured it was healthier for all of them, and it certainly helped that the Cline family was so creative and talented in the kitchen.

"That pizza smells *so* good," said Pippa. She turned to Gia. "The garlic you added really makes it."

"I like it too," said Gia, trying to chew with her mouth closed.

"How is Peaches?" asked Britt. "Did she eat her dinner?"

"Well, she is resting, so she hasn't touched it yet. But she did drink a lot of water. Now that I think about it, I believe I am the hungry one."

Pippa sat down in the rocking chair with her pizza. Britt and Gia swayed on the porch swing. Bilberry was sleeping near Britt's feet. They sat in silence for a while, chewing happily.

Pippa's phone vibrated and started playing "I Heard It through the Grapevine"—*an oldie but a goodie*, Pops liked to say. The girls danced along to the music in their seats.

"That's a fun ringtone," said Gia.

"Thanks! It's actually a text from Pops. He stole my phone and set it up that way secretly," she laughed. "You know him and grapes."

"They sure have been gone a long time," said Britt.

"Yeah," said Pippa, "they have...."

She reached into her pocket, swiped her finger across the phone, and read Pops's message:

Pops: Finally out of the ER. Ryan had stitches. He has hunger pain more than head pain ;-) We will grab a bite out. How is Peaches? Be home after 10 p.m. Luv, Pops

Pippa wrote back:

Pippa: Gia & Britt r here. No pups yet. Peaches resting. We made GF pizza, yum. C U soon. <3 PIPS

She put the phone back into her pocket.

"Ryan is doing okay. They're heading out to get some dinner for themselves."

"Oh good!" mumbled the girls through mouthfuls of food.

The sun was setting, the pizza tasted yummy, and Pippa felt ready for anything.

"I love the long summer days in the Northwest," she said. "I love Hawaii too, but summer feels extra special here in Oregon, after the long dark winters."

"Do you think your family will ever move back there?" asked Britt.

"To Hawaii?! I hope not!" said Gia. "We besties have to stick together!"

"No," said Pippa thoughtfully. "Even though my mom grew up on the Big Island, she loves our little Wigglers Island here. It's been in my dad's family forever! And, with the dog and grape businesses going so well, I don't think my parents would ever move. We like to visit our family in Hawaii, though. They throw us a big party called a luau each time we visit, and my cousin, Erik, is a dolphin trainer at one of the big resorts."

"I want to go to Hawaii with you and do the hula dance," Gia shouted. "Maybe we can swim with the dolphins too!"

"Me too," pleaded Britt. She stood up and wiggled her hips. "Dance with me, Bilberry!" She patted her shoulders three times and Bilberry jumped up and placed his two gigantic paws on her shoulders. They moved in a circle around the porch. The other two fell over laughing at the sight of Bilberry's hula.

"Yes," said Pippa. "I want you both to come with us next time. But hold the hula."

They giggled even harder.

"Hmm," said Pippa. "Peaches will have her puppies soon, and hopefully Mom and Pops let me keep one. It will take a while to train the pup, so I don't think Hawaii will happen any time soon. We will have to do our best, dancing around the treehouse for now. I will be busy with my new puppy."

"Yippee!" said Gia excitedly.

Britt stayed quiet. Britt knew that Pippa wanted to keep a puppy, and she also knew that it was not likely. Dogs took a lot of work and needed lots of love, attention, and training. Pippa's parents were busy with the farm, work, and family. One more pet to take care of could be a big challenge.

"The sun is almost down," said Britt, changing the subject.

"Oooo I can see orange, pink, and purple. I will ask my mom to make a sunset cupcake just like this." She took a sip of cool water and then added, "What do you two think?"

Pippa thought for a moment. She swallowed her last bite of pizza, licked her fingers, and climbed onto the porch swing between her two friends.

"Well, the colors are pretty and would make a nice cupcake," she mused, "but I like the clouds with weird shapes. I can see a bunny with floppy ears right *there*." She pointed to a cloud high up above them.

Gia laughed.

"You're just still thinking of your cupcake," she grinned. "The fluffy puffs are like cotton candy. Oh, do you see how dark purple *those* are?"

Britt stared up at the purple giant storm cloud.

"Looks like a storm is brewing," she said.

They sat outside, rocking in the porch swing and talking until the sun disappeared. The humming crickets started to sing. Gia shuddered as the wind kicked up. Rain sprinkles began to fall.

"The rain has arrived," she announced. "We should go inside before it starts to pour." As they stood up, a flash of light lit up the sky.

"Lightning!" they squealed together. "One thousand one,

one thousand two," they counted in unison. A loud drumming sound startled the girls, and they giggled nervously.

"Thunder!"

"The lightning is close by," said Pippa. Rain started to fall in heavier drops. The sound rattled the covered porch. "Quick, let's get inside!"

Pippa took Britt's arm and led her inside the house. Bilberry followed. Gia was right behind. Lightning flashed again, and before they had time to count, thunder clapped. There was another flash, and a loud boom echoed a drum-like rhythm.

Britt held her hands over her sensitive ears while they all screamed.

"Ohhhh that is LOUD!" she said. "I need earplugs."

In an instant, there was another flash of light, a boom, and a rumble. Then, darkness surrounded them. All of the lights in the house were out, and rain pounded on the rooftop.

"I can't see!" cried Pippa. She stopped in her tracks. She blinked a few times to let her eyes adjust to the darkness. "I can't hear anything either, except the raindrops bouncing off the roof. Is everyone okay?"

"I'm fine," said Gia, calmly. "Do you know where your parents keep the flashlights?"

"We have a lantern in the top left-hand cupboard above the

counter," said Pippa. "I put fresh batteries in it last week. Don't forget, we have flashlights on our phones too, as long as our phones are charged."

"I'm good," said Britt. "No big change for me. Here, Pippa, take my arm, and I'll lead *you* to the table."

Pippa reached out, and Britt found her. Pippa was quickly seated and fished out her phone while Gia felt her way to the kitchen counter. Pippa was thankful that Britt could easily find her way through the dark. A circle of light appeared as Gia switched on the lantern. Their faces lit up in the dark. Bilberry had made himself comfortable on Peaches's dog bed.

"Oh my gosh . . . Peaches!" cried Pippa. "I hope she isn't afraid of the thunder . . . or the dark."

The girls made their way to the delivery den and opened the door to peek inside. Pippa held up the lantern, and to her surprise, saw Peaches relaxed and licking a puppy.

"They're here," whispered Pippa, wide-eyed. She counted to herself. "Looks like five or six red-and-caramel-colored puppies." She sighed happily.

"Ahhhhhhh, cute," said Britt. She sat down on the floor and used her senses to absorb the experience. "I can hear them making a cute whimpering sound."

"What's this?" asked Pippa. Underneath the last puppy, hidden from sight, she felt a little warm ball of fur. She gently moved her hands underneath it without disturbing Peaches and lifted it up. She gasped.

"Another puppy!" she told Britt and Gia. "Looks like an apricot. A red apricot. Wait, I can't tell if it is breathing."

The YouTube video played back in her head. *Can I help this puppy?* she wondered to herself. *Can I remember all of the instructions?*

Chapter Four

Lucky Puppy

"Is it alive?" asked Gia.

Pippa brought the puppy up to her ear to listen.

"I can't hear anything," she said.

"Quickly," said Britt, "rub its tummy and chest."

"That's right...," said Pippa, remembering her mom's video. She started to rub the puppy. After a long minute went by, she looked up at the other two.

"I don't think it's helping," she said sadly.

"Keep it up," said Gia. "I remember one of our foals did the same thing. Sometimes it takes a while."

Another minute went by, but it felt like ten. And then, all of a sudden, the puppy started to move. Pippa felt the chest move first and then heard a gasp of air. She felt life rush into the little puppy.

"It's breathing!" she said thankfully. "I can't believe it. It's a miracle!"

Gia recalled what her parents did with new foals.

"Place it near Peaches, and they can bond," she said. "Then Peaches will know the puppy is hers."

"Right," said Pippa. She snuggled the seventh puppy in between two of the red pups and watched as Peaches began to lick and start to care for it.

"This puppy is smaller than the rest, and it is the only one who looks like Peaches," Pippa noticed. "Three red, three caramels, and one apricot puppy. We won't need a color-coded collar around this one!"

"He is a lucky puppy," said Britt.

She took a cloth to wipe each puppy clean and then handed them one by one to Pippa. Pippa weighed and measured them. Gia wrote brief descriptions of each puppy and snapped their collars on. Peaches was resting calmly and drinking water again, though she still had not touched her dinner. Everyone enjoyed the peaceful moment, watching the pups with their mother. The sight of new life was a sweet and beautiful.

Pippa broke the silence.

"Ya know...," she said, "I think I have a name for puppy number seven."

"What?" said Britt and Gia in unison.

"Lucky!" suggested Britt.

"Sunshine?" guessed Gia.

"What about Strudel?" grinned Pippa. "After all, today Britt brought my dad a peach strudel, and this Strudel was made from Peaches."

Britt laughed.

"I still like Sunshine," said Gia, "but I do love to eat the Cline's peach strudel." She looked off dreamily.

"I have another idea," said Pippa. "I can spell Strudel to go with the breed."

Gia and Britt both made funny faces.

"What do you mean?" asked Britt.

"Well, in place of the s-t-r-u-d-e-l spelling, we can spell it S-T-R-O-O-D-L-E!" Pippa explained.

The three girls giggled and said it together: "Stroodle the Labradoodle!"

They formed a half circle and sat with their legs crossed to watch the puppies get a delicious meal from their mother and snuggle. Britt was the first to notice that one of the pups was whimpering.

"Who's unhappy?" asked Britt.

"It looks like Stroodle," said Gia. She looked at Pippa to confirm who it was.

"It *is* Stroodle," said Pippa. "Poor thing isn't getting enough to drink."

Gia came up with a plan.

"We will take turns watching the pups all night," she said. "Then we will be sure that Stroodle and all the pups are getting enough mother's milk."

"I'll take the first watch," said Britt. "I'm not tired at all and usually stay up late anyway."

"I'll do the second one," said Gia. "I can fall asleep *and* wake up quickly, so it's no problem." She yawned.

Pippa felt lucky to have such good friends who would help her with the puppies through the night.

"Thank you both so much!" she exclaimed. "You are my besties. The best friends that anyone could have."

She held out her pinky finger, and Gia and Britt did the same. They locked them together and in unison said, "Best buddies forever." They hugged. At that moment, the electricity buzzed back on. Peaches perked her ears at the sound of one of the golf carts approaching the house.

It was after 10 p.m. when Pops carried a sleeping Ryan through the front door. He took him upstairs to his bedroom, tucked him in, and then joined the girls in the den.

"It looks like everything went well," said a pooped-out Pops. He slumped into a chair. "Shall I make some popcorn, and you can tell me all about your adventure?"

The girls exchanged an excited look and smiled.

"Pops," Pippa announced, "have we got a story for you!"

Chapter Five

Operation Keep Stroodle

P ippa Pinkerton picked up the apricot puppy with the orange collar, the smallest of the litter. His right front paw was a tuft of white, and his face was starting to show some white patches on his brows and under his chin. Stroodle the Labradoodle was Pippa's favorite. She placed the little guy up against his mother, alongside his six sisters—three red and three caramel pups—to get some breakfast before their midmorning nap.

I can't believe it has been almost seven weeks, she thought. *All the female pups weigh around eleven pounds, and Stroodle already weighs close to ten. He's catching up. Yay, Stroodle!*

Each morning, she cleaned the puppy pen and made sure that Peaches was fed and that the water bowl was cleaned and filled. Pippa spent hours watching the puppies play together. She watched carefully as her mother began to potty train them. She helped out by taking the pups outside every three hours to do their business. She praised them and offered a small treat each time they did. Their personalities were blossoming before her eyes, and she and her besties named the pups accordingly.

Pippa named the biggest red pup Reddy, mostly because she was always first: first to eat, first to march over to Pippa for love and attention, and first to fall asleep. Always ready, but because of her rich red hair color, they spelled it Reddy. Reddy wore a green collar. Green for GO!

The second red puppy was super playful and had white-tipped ears and a white-tipped tail. Britt gave her the name Tippy. Tippy wore a white collar. The third and last red puppy—the only one Gia named—was called Ruby. Ruby had four white paws, was more patient than the rest, and had a gentle nature. Like Stroodle, Ruby looked at people as if she understood everything they were saying. Ruby wore a red collar.

The fourth and fifth puppies were twins. Britt called them Polly and Lolly Pups. Their colors were caramel with white around their brown noses and mouths. Thanks to their collars, everyone knew which was which. Polly wore dark blue, and Lolly wore light blue. Otherwise, they were impossible to tell apart!

The last caramel puppy had two white spots around each eye. Pippa named her Ku'uipo. Ku'uipo was what Tutu, their

Hawaiian grandmother, called her and Ryan. It meant sweetheart. *Boy*, thought Pippa to herself, *if Tutu knew Ryan's real personality, she would call him Mischief, not Sweetheart.*

Pippa's mom knocked gently on the door and entered.

"Hello, my little darling," said Mrs. Pinkerton, hugging Pippa. "Honey, I am so relieved and happy the pups were born at the beginning of summer vacation. You've been such a great help to me and your dad. Stepping in like you have done has given me more time to prepare for the fall dog show."

Pippa smiled and lifted Stroodle up to her mom.

"Oh, Mom, I just love them so much," she beamed. "But I don't think I could've done it without my besties. They made the whole thing fun and were there for it all. And look! Of all the puppies, Stroodle loves me the most. He follows me everywhere!"

"Well, don't get too attached, Pippa," warned Mrs. Pinkerton. "We have a lot on our plate. I don't want to add more to it right now."

Pippa frowned.

"But Mo-ommmm," she pleaded, "I really want my own dog to train and care for. I can do it!"

"Pippa, it's not just that," said Mrs. Pinkerton patiently. "I know you are capable. We have a long waiting list for puppies. Some of these people have been waiting for months. Maybe with the next litter, you can keep and train one."

Pippa knew that Frog Pond Doodles were well known throughout the country. Her mom was a top breeder, well-respected and admired. There was a high demand for her designer Doodles.

"I know, Mom," said Pippa, "but I really feel like Stroodle is meant to be mine. I've been with him since his first breath of life!"

Mrs. Pinkerton's face turned stern.

"Pippa," she scolded, "we don't need a new puppy right now. The answer is no. No upside down. No sideways and flat-out NO."

Pippa knew her mom was trying to be kind, even if she was being firm. And yes, they were already a busy family. Their plate *was* full.

But isn't there always room for dessert? she thought. Stroodle was hers!

"Mom, I'm going to find a way to make Stroodle worth keeping," she said. "I will figure something out. I will change your mind."

Pippa's mom sighed.

"I haven't heard you talk like this in a while. You really want this, don't you?"

Pippa nodded.

"Well," said Mrs. Pinkerton, "I admire your spirit. Come up with some really great reasons as to why *we* have to have a new pup, and Pops and I will talk it over." She surveyed her daughter. "You have to change *his* mind too, you know."

"Thank you, thank you, thank you!" Pippa squealed in excitement. "OPERATION KEEP STROODLE! I will get to work on it and brainstorm with my besties." She started to run toward her bedroom.

"Wait just a moment, young lady," Mrs. Pinkerton said. Pippa turned and looked back, one foot still partly off the ground. "Before you have your friends over, are your Helpful Home Projects done?"

"Not yet," Pippa admitted, *bouncing* up and down. She could barely keep in her excitement.

"Please pick up your room, empty the dishwasher, and take out the trash," Mrs. Pinkerton said, all in one breath. "Also, text the first five people on the application list. They have all been waiting since I first contacted them. Tell them the pups had their second round of vaccinations two weeks ago and are ready for their new home."

Pippa nodded and ran back to her mom.

"Okay!" she said, hugging Mrs. Pinkerton around the middle. "The answer is yes. Yes upside down and yes sideways, and flat-out YES! I can juggle lots of things in one day."

Her mom laughed.

"That's called multi-tasking, and it is a good trait to have," she said, patting her daughter on the head. "Oh, don't forget—Mikala is coming for your piano lessons this afternoon."

Mrs. Cline dropped Britt and Gia off at the old Frog Pond house around 3:00 p.m. As usual, Britt brought gluten-free cupcakes, and Gia brought chocolate almond milk to drink.

"Today, I bring you spice flavored cupcakes decorated with vanilla cream frosting," Britt announced, bowing to her friends. Pippa and Gia curtseyed back, giggling.

"Each one has a different emoji face," said Britt proudly.

"YUMMY YUM!" squealed Pippa. "I choose the WOW emoji."

They ate their cupcakes outside while taking turns on the tire swing under the chestnut tree. Pippa told her friends about OPERATION KEEP STROODLE and the tasks her mom had given her. In between swings, Pippa went through the applications. She sent a text message to the first four people at the top of the list, inviting them for a visit. She paused when she read the fifth line.

"Hey...," said Pippa, looking up, "Gia, your parents are on the list! I'm about to send your mom a text to come and visit."

Gia laughed.

"I wondered when you would see our names," she said slyly, spinning on the swing. "Can you guess which puppy I want?"

"Ruby! I know how much you love her," Pippa said, hitting send on the text to Gia's mom. "Stroodle and Ruby play well together. That will be so cool to have them grow up together. We can train them and take them everywhere we go!"

"We *have* to get your parents to see that keeping Stroodle is a *must*," said Gia. "I think we can come up with some great reasons."

Pippa nodded and got out her pad of paper.

"Ya know, Pippa," said Britt, "at first I didn't think there was much hope of you keeping a puppy, your family being so busy and all . . . but now I'm with you 100%. I think if we can come up with some ideas to convince your parents, we have a really good chance! Besides, Peaches and Bilberry could actually watch Stroodle and Ruby grow up!"

"Think how amazing that'd be, huh buddy?" she added to Bilberry, who was splayed out on Peaches's kitchen bed chewing a toy.

"Aw, yeah, that'd be so special," said Gia.

"Then let's start working on the list!" said Pippa, more determined now than ever. "Okay, where should we . . ."

Her voice trailed off at the sound of the bridge bell singing out.

"That must be Mikala," smiled Britt.

Piano lessons were always at Pippa's home because everyone liked to play on their old Steinway. Britt especially loved the rich, full sound.

"Hi, piano players," called Mikala as she pulled up in a rose-colored cart. "How are the cutest pups in the world doing?"

The girls ran over to meet and greet her with a hug. Britt was holding onto Pippa's sleeve. The two could run fast since Britt was used to Pippa leading her.

"The pups are doing great," panted Britt, nearly out of breath. "We are excited that you are getting one!"

"I brought my deposit to give to your mom," Mikala told Pippa. "Thanks for texting me."

They all walked together into the house.

"Whose turn is it to go first today?"

Gia raised her hand.

"It's my turn," she said. "I have my music on the piano already."

Pippa's mom was coming down the stairs, and Mikala reached into her purse for the puppy deposit.

"Hi, Suzanne!" she called. "I have the deposit. May I take a quick peek at the pups before I start the lessons?"

Pippa's mom smiled.

"You know the way, Mikala," she said, pointing to the delivery den. "They have one more vet check, and then you can take your pup home next week."

"Can you girls warm up while I take care of this business?"

asked Mikala as she walked toward the den. "This will take just a minute."

Pippa turned to Gia and Britt.

"I think she will choose Reddy because every time she visits, Reddy always runs up to her," she whispered. "Well, Mikala gets a puppy, . . . Gia, you get Ruby, . . . and I get Stroodle. I have to think positive."

"First, a list of all the things that Stroodle can help with," reminded Gia. "Your parents have to see that Stroodle is worth keeping."

Mikala came back into the room with a big smile on her face.

"I have chosen the one who is all red," she announced to the group. "It was so easy! She came running up to me again, frolicking and jumping into my arms."

The girls grinned at each other knowingly.

"We call her Reddy, R-E-D-D-Y," spelled Pippa. "She's always first for everything!"

"I like that name," said Mikala. She directed Gia to the piano. "Everybody ready?"

Oh yes, Pippa thought. *I am ready. I am ready to put my plan to keep Stroodle into action. OPERATION KEEP STROODLE!*

Chapter Six

What Now?

It was morning. The sun shone brightly through the windows, and the birds tweeted loudly from the branches of the chestnut tree. Pippa was cleaning up the doggie den and humming a song her mom had taught her when she was little: a Hawaiian lullaby called "Ke Ao Nani, The Beautiful World."

When she finished, she plopped onto the floor. She had a couple more Helpful Home Projects left to do, but she decided that first it was time to take a cuddle break with Stroodle. Stroodle was enjoying his favorite activity of chomping on Pippa's braids when Ryan stomped in. He was dressed in jeans, a light blue polo shirt, and hiking boots. He wore a blue scarf with a green frog in the corner that identified him as a member of the Blue Frog Squad. He had his Blue Frog patch on his backpack too.

"I'm ready for camp. Mom's waiting in the cart," he said. His ever-changing eye color shimmered bright green that morning, and his head of thick, scruffy brown hair was awaiting any bird looking to build a nest. Stroodle ran up to him for a love pat, and Ryan added a snuggle.

"I love Stroodle so much," he cooed. "Please find a way to keep him. *Pleeeease*, Pippa?"

"I'm working on it, Ryan," Pippa assured him. "I'm meeting with Britt and Gia at C3 for lunch and cupcakes. We've been thinking up job possibilities for Stroodle, and we already have some interesting ideas."

Ryan began to play with the puppies while Pippa collected the puppy poop. Pippa noticed how gentle he was with the puppies. She heard him whisper into Stroodle's ear.

"Stroodle, do you want to be our puppy?" Ryan asked sweetly, crouching down and peering closely at him.

"Okay Ryan it's time to get to camp. You don't want to be late," Pippa said to him in a voice that sounded a lot like Mrs. Pinkerton. "Make sure the lights are off. Have fun at summer camp today, and don't forget to wear sunscreen!"

She followed Ruby who wandered outside of the puppy den.

"Oh, and tell Mom the bridge gate is open for Gia's mom," she added.

"Okay!" Ryan answered back. "Pippa, can you bring me home a chocolate cupcake? Pretty pretty pleeeeeease?"

"You got it," said Pippa. She scooted Ruby back to the others and picked up the sack with puppy poop.

Ryan picked up something off the floor and put it inside his backpack. He turned the light off and closed the door to the doggie den. Pippa walked him out and watched her mom and Ryan drive away as a second cart headed toward the house. It was Gia's mom with the girls. Everyone waved. Pippa put her backpack on.

"HUGAPALOOZA," she said to herself, looking around. "I don't want to forget anything..."

Thirty minutes later, the girls were sitting at their usual table at Cline's Café and Cupcakes with their usual sandwiches. Pippa had ordered turkey and cranberry, no tomatoes. Gia's was a Club Sandwich because she loved bacon on *everything*. Britt's was chicken salad that she helped her mom make that morning. Mrs. Cline walked over to their table. She set down a bowl of peppered potato chips and some apple slices for the girls to share, along with three tall glasses of water.

"Thanks, Mom," said Britt, taking a sip of her water. "We choose our sugar wisely," she added to her friends, grinning. They clinked their glasses together.

Mrs. Cline insisted on giving the girls water each time they came to C3 because it was healthier than sugary soda. She knew they were bound to eat at least one of her famous cupcakes, and water was part of their bargain.

"I'm so excited that you're bringing a pup home!" Pippa said to Gia, trying not to speak with her mouth full. "*And* you got your pick too. Ruby the red."

Gia had a big smile on her face.

"I'm beyond excited! I want to tell everyone!" she shouted. The room got quiet. The girls looked around, and they all laughed.

"Whoops," continued Gia, munching on her chips. She lowered her voice and turned to Pippa. "Okay, now we have to make sure that you get your pick. Let's get to work on our list."

Gia took out her iPad and pulled up a file named Oodles of Stroodle.

"I think Stroodle would make an amazing service dog for the blind, like my Bilberry," said Britt. She glanced down at Bilberry asleep at her feet. "Or, what about a dog training assistant for your mom?"

"How about a show dog model?" suggested Gia. "Many people go to dog shows before they make a decision to buy a dog.

He would make a great representative for your family business."

Pippa sipped her water and nodded at these ideas.

"I was thinking of a comfort dog that can visit kids and elderly people in hospitals," she said. "Also, we can teach Stroodle different tricks to entertain kids at birthday parties."

Her eyes lit up.

"Hey! Stroodle can help Ryan stay out of trouble in the summertime," she giggled. "Like Nana in Peter Pan."

"Well, Nana didn't exactly keep *those* kids out of trouble," Gia pointed out.

"I bet Stroodle could at least distract Ryan from playing the Prince of Trees," said Britt dramatically, saying the last words in Ryan's high-pitched, five-year-old tone. "That's worth something, isn't it?"

Gia and Pippa laughed.

"Definitely," said Pippa.

"I think we have some great ideas," said Gia, "and we only have to get Pippa's parents on board with *one* of them."

She read the list aloud:

*** Service dog for the blind

*** Show dog model and representative for family business

*** Comfort dog

*** Entertainer-at-parties dog

*** Trainer-assistant dog

*** Keep-Ryan-out-of-trouble dog

"Can you email me that?" Pippa asked Gia. "I think I'll show it to my parents, so they know I am serious."

"Absolutely," said Gia. "With pleasure."

The girls chose their cupcakes from the glass case and went back to their table.

"Yummmm!" Gia said gleefully. "Between us, we have chocolate, strawberry, and vanilla. That's called Neapolitan. At least the ice cream is called that."

"Oh! Thanks for reminding me," said Pippa. "I need a chocolate cupcake for Ryan to go."

Pippa's phone barked like a dog.

"My mom's texting me," she said. She took her phone out of her pocket and swiped to view the message:

Mom: Pippa do u have Stroodle with you? :-/

"What?" Pippa said aloud. She stared at the message, confused. "Why would I have Stroodle with me?" She quickly started texting her mom back.

Gia and Britt sat up in their seats.

"Did I just hear that correctly?" asked Britt. "It sounded like you said, 'Why would Stroodle be with you?'"

Pippa shook her head for a second as she focused and texted her mom:

Pippa: No, mom. What now? :-0

What Now?

Mom: I am driving to pick u up now. Be ready pls.
Pippa: K

"My mom is on her way to pick us up. Stroodle is missing!" she said, beginning to tear up.

What could have happened? Pippa wondered. *How did you get out of the den, Stroodle? Why did you leave your sisters?*

"Don't worry yet," comforted Gia. "We will all help look for Stroodle." She put her arm around Pippa.

A minute later, Mrs. Pinkerton's car pulled up in front of C3. Britt ran over to her mom at the counter and quickly explained the situation. Mrs. Cline agreed to let Britt help hunt for Stroodle too. Britt's excellent hearing could certainly help lead them to the missing puppy. Pippa led Britt to the car, and Gia held the door open as Pippa wiped her eyes on her sleeve. As they drove, Gia's arm rested on Pippa's shoulder, and Britt held her hand.

"We will be there soon," said Britt. "We will find Stroodle and get to the bottom of this."

Pippa crossed her fingers and closed her eyes to picture them finding Stroodle safe and sound. *Where could Stroodle be? How did he get out of the doggie den when the others didn't?* Pippa's heart began to thump.

Chapter Seven

The Search

P ippa tried to remember exactly what she had done before leaving Wigglers Island for C3. *I cleaned out the doggie den, took the trash out...*

"RYAN!" she screamed. The other two jumped. "Ryan came into the den to cuddle with Stroodle before leaving for camp," she explained, "so I asked him to turn the lights out and close the den door when he left."

"Then he must have forgotten to close the door, and Stroodle wandered out," finished Gia. "Stroodle has to be around there somewhere. He's just a pup."

"When I get my hands on him," said Pippa, frustrated. "Why can't he just listen to me? Just once. UGH!"

"Remain calm, girls," said Mrs. Pinkerton. "We will find Stroodle."

Although Mrs. Pinkerton's voice was steady and calm, a concerned look on her face revealed her own worry. Pippa stared out the window. *Not long now,* she thought. *I can see the gate.*

The car pulled into the long garage next to the bridge. Pippa jumped out of the car and put the code in at the gate. They all ran over the bridge to the rose colored golf cart. Mrs. Pinkerton drove them back to the house.

"Ok," directed Pippa. "Gia, can you check upstairs? Britt, the kitchen and back porch. Mom, the doggie den. I will search outside."

Everyone agreed. They all went directly to their spots to start looking. Their voices echoed as they called out, "Stroooooodle! Stroodle, where are you?"

Mrs. Pinkerton noticed that Peaches was also looking for her apricot puppy.

"We will find him, Peaches," she said soothingly, scratching Peaches behind the ears. "Stroodle will be back with you and your pups soon." She crossed her fingers.

Meanwhile, Pippa looked in the grass, the storage shed, the grape house, behind the rocks, around the treehouse, and finally, down on the dock. Nothing. It was the same for Gia, who checked the second level and the attic. Britt couldn't find Stroodle in the kitchen or on the porch either. They all met up by the treehouse, empty-handed.

"Now what?" said Britt. "Stroodle doesn't seem to be here."

"We need to expand our search to the whole island," said Mrs. Pinkerton. Then her phone beeped.

"Hello?" she said into the phone. "Yes, this is Suzanne Pinkerton. Yes, I'm Ryan's mother."

The girls exchanged looks, and Pippa whispered, "Mom, who is..."

Mrs. Pinkerton shook her head and put a finger to her lips. She stepped a few feet away from them. Pippa tapped her foot impatiently, and the three girls waited, all watching Mrs. Pinkerton closely.

"Yes..., yes...," they heard her say. "Stroodle *what?* Oh no! Oh gosh, I'm so sorry. Thank you. I'll be right there."

She hung up the phone and turned to the girls.

"Mom?" said Pippa. "Who was that, and what do they know about Stroodle?"

"That was Big Rob, Ryan's camp director," said Mrs. Pinkerton slowly, taking a deep breath in. "It turns out Ryan brought Stroodle with him this morning to camp. Apparently, he brought him for sharing."

"Well, that's great," said Britt.

"What?!" said Pippa and Gia together.

"No, I mean, look on the bright side," Britt explained. "Stroodle has been found! Let's go get him."

"There's a problem, though," said Mrs. Pinkerton. "Now Stroodle and Ryan are *both* missing. He must have heard Big Rob tell the counselor that Stroodle was too young to be away from his mother because, apparently, he took Stroodle and hid somewhere at camp."

"Oh no!" Gia gasped.

"Oh no is right," snarled Pippa. "That Ryan. When I get my hands on him..."

"You'll what?" Mrs. Pinkerton asked, raising her eyebrows. "He is only five years old and doesn't understand a lot of this. Only that he wanted to share his new best friend at camp."

"He should have at least asked permission," said Gia matter-of-factly. "I just hope they both are all right."

Pippa nodded, her nostrils flaring. Mrs. Pinkerton put her arm around Pippa's shoulders and steered her toward the golf cart.

"Well, back to the car we go," said Britt. "Looks like we have another hunt ahead of us at the day camp."

The team rode in the cart to the bridge and then ran back to the car. Everyone tried to remain calm as they drove to camp.

Pippa closed her eyes while Britt and Gia discussed who should do what when they arrived.

"I will find Stroodle and Ryan safe and sound. I will find Stroodle and Ryan safe and sound," Pippa repeated to herself in a whisper.

"We're here," said Gia. "Pippa, wake up."

The car was approaching the camp. Pippa had been deep in her thoughts, imagining what terrible things might have happened to Stroodle and Ryan. She opened her eyes and saw they were in a parking lot in the woods. They all got out of the car. Forest Wood Village Camp was located on the north end of Frog Pond Lake. They offered a wide range of activities, from water sports to robotics, technology, and inventions. The centerpiece of the swim area was a floating dock with a huge air mattress for kids to lie down on or jump off of. Big Rob, the camp director, was at the entrance ready to greet them.

"Suzanne!" he called, extending his hand in welcome.

"Hi, Big Rob," Pippa's mom said hurriedly, shaking his hand. "Any news?"

"Not yet," he said. He addressed the group. "We have a search and rescue team who have been out there searching for Ryan and Stroodle for the past hour. They are well-equipped and familiar with the grounds. We have seen how well Ryan can swim, so the team checked the lake and lake house first. He wasn't there."

"Thank you so much," Pippa's mom choked up. Tears clouded her eyes. She heaved a sigh. "Yes, Ryan is an excellent swimmer for a five-year-old. We started him before he could walk. *And* he also knows that he should not go near the water without an adult."

She sniffed and blinked the tears away. Pippa put her arm around her.

"Good," said Big Rob encouragingly. "That's very good. You have prepared him well. Don't worry, Suzanne. We will find them. We have never lost a camper in all of the years we've been open. Did you get a hold of Professor Pinkerton?"

"He is on his way."

"We want to help too!" Pippa piped in. "Big Rob, these are my best friends, Gia and Britt."

Big Rob looked to Mrs. Pinkerton for approval.

In control now and ready to cope with the task at hand, Pippa's mom placed her hands on Pippa's shoulders.

"Pippa, is your cell phone battery charged?"

"Yes, and the volume is all the way up," said Pippa, double-checking this as she spoke.

"Okay then," said Mrs. Pinkerton. "Stick together and listen carefully to Big Rob's instructions."

"Girls, you can start at the west side of camp," Big Rob directed. "The rest of us will meet you there as soon as we search the other areas."

"We don't have time to waste," said Gia. "It looks like a lot of area to cover."

"Here, Britt," said Pippa, offering Britt her arm. "Let's go find Ryan and Stroodle!"

Britt took hold of Pippa, and the three girls began to run to the west side of camp.

"Be careful!" shouted Mrs. Pinkerton. "Stay together!"

"We will!" Pippa shouted back. "If he's out here, we will find him."

Pippa wrinkled her face and took a deep breath in. She was determined.

Chapter Eight

The Rescue

The west side of Forest Wood Village Camp was surrounded by rolling hills covered mostly in pine trees and a few scattered apple trees left over from a farmer's orchard many years before. A rocky beach bordered the lake, which that day was still, clear, and shallow. Logs and twigs floated offshore, giving the impression that beavers were busy rearranging them in preparation for winter. Except for the millions of gnats flying and buzzing around, the bright blue sky and soft breeze were ideal for the search.

This part of camp was usually off-limits. A high chain-link fence identified the boundary, separating camp from the water's edge. Pippa, Gia, and Britt started their hunt calling out loudly in all directions.

"Ryyyyyaaaan! Stroooooooodle!"

Pippa surveyed the land all around them.

"This is a gigantic area," she observed, "and the clock is ticking."

The girls had been searching for a while. Britt bent down and peered under thick bushes, while Gia peered upward to the tree branches Ryan could easily climb. Pippa noticed a drainpipe in the distance. It looked as tall as she was and as wide as a truck. It was about a football field away and on the other side of the fence.

She pointed out the pipe to the others.

"That looks like a really good place to hide," she told them. "I know it's out of bounds, but I've never known anything like a fence to stop Ryan."

"What are we waiting for?" shouted Gia from a ditch near the fence. "Let's check it out!"

Pippa turned to Britt.

"Britt, will you stay here as our lookout?"

Britt hesitated. She remembered Pippa's mom asking them to stay together.

"Ok . . .," she said slowly. "Uh, how long do you think you'll be gone?"

Britt didn't like to be left alone in places she wasn't familiar with. Her ears were sharp, and she had her glasses, but without Bilberry as her guide, the west side of camp felt wild and frightening.

"If we aren't back in twenty minutes," said Pippa, "call my mom. And if you get too scared, call me and Gia, and I will come back to get you."

"I'll be fine," Britt assured Pippa, putting on a brave face. "You two get over there."

Pippa gave her a quick hug and then darted off with Gia toward the pipe. They were quickly out of earshot and sight.

When Pippa and Gia reached the big fence, they peered around the lower half, looking for gaps.

"Well, I don't see any holes yet . . .," said Pippa, carefully running her hands along the chain link. "Gia, do you see anything?"

Gia, the tallest of her friends, craned her neck for a better look at the long fence line.

"Not yet. The fence looks brand new. I don't think we are going to . . ."

Gia trailed off and suddenly ran toward a part of the fence a little way down.

"Pippa!" she yelled excitedly. "Over here!"

Pippa ran over to Gia and saw where she was pointing. Part of the fence had been torn open, and it looked like they could both easily squeeze their way through. Gia went first.

"Look, a piece of a Blue Frog Squad camp t-shirt!" she said, unhooking a frayed cloth from the fence. "Isn't Ryan in the Blue Frog Squad?"

She crawled through the gap with the cloth in her hand.

"Yep! He is," Pippa said eagerly, following Gia on all fours. "I think we are onto something. Ouch!"

The sleeve of Pippa's t-shirt had caught on a sharp, loose edge. She was able to unhook it without tearing it, but her shoulder skin was scratched.

"There are a lot of berry bushes with thorns over here," said Gia, standing up. "Be careful."

Pippa shrugged.

"Too late."

Pippa stayed low, surveying the rows and rows of wild blackberry bushes. Then, suddenly, Pippa saw something orange and out of place stuck in the brush. *Could that be Stroodle?!* She gasped and beckoned to Gia. They moved closer, and there he was, tangled up, trapped, and unable to move!

"He's whimpering," said Gia.

Quickly, Pippa freed Stroodle from the thorny bush.

The Rescue

"Oh, Stroodle," she said, clutching him to her chest. She had to work to contain his anxious, wriggling body. "It's okay. I'm here. You are going to be just fine."

It took Stroodle a minute to calm down, and then he licked her face as if to say, *Where have you been? I'm so happy I found you!*

Pippa held up her little puppy so that he faced her and talked directly to him. Stroodle immediately began chewing one of her braids.

"Can you please tell us where Ryan is?" Pippa asked him.

Stroodle licked Pippa's face again and sniffed at the torn piece of t-shirt she had in her hand. He started to squirm. Pippa could barely hang onto him.

"I think he wants you to put him down," said Gia, still standing. "Come over here where he can walk without getting caught in the brush again."

Pippa did as Gia suggested, and immediately Stroodle started running to the lake.

"Hey, Stroodle, slow down!" called Gia. "C'mon, let's follow him."

The girls followed Stroodle through the berry brush and over the logs toward the lake.

"I hope he doesn't jump into the water!" gasped Pippa. "Wait a minute . . . he's changing direction and heading to that drainpipe!"

"We are right behind you, Stroodle," Gia called out. "Pippa. I think he's going *into* the drainpipe!"

Pippa called out Ryan's name. There was no answer. They approached the drainpipe right after Stroodle went in and peered inside. Even though it was a sunny afternoon, the pipe was dark as night and very damp. They heard a soft meowing sound coming from deep inside.

"Is that a cat?" Gia whispered, looking warily at Pippa.

Pippa recognized the meowing sound as Ryan crying. She knew that sound well.

"It's gotta be Ryan," she whispered back.

Pippa walked toward the sound slowly with one hand on the wall of the pipe. Gia followed. It was impossible to see. At that moment, Pippa wished Britt was with them. She did a lot better in these kinds of situations.

After what felt like minutes, Pippa's eyes finally adjusted, and there was Stroodle, licking her little brother's red, dirty face.

"Ryan!" Pippa cried. She bent down to him. "Are you okay?"

Ryan looked up. His sister and Gia were staring at him.

"Oh, Pippa," he said, tears dripping from his eyes, "I fell asleep. And when I woke up, Stroodle was gone. I'm so sorry... I just wanted to share Stroodle for show-and-tell today. Am I in gigantic trouble?"

The Rescue

He was breathing heavily and looked so sad and scared. All of Pippa's anger evaporated.

"It's going to be okay, Ryan," she told him, giving him a hug. "But we were really worried. Why didn't you ask Mom or me? We probably would have just told you to wait another week, and we could all take Stroodle together."

"That's why I didn't ask you," Ryan said matter-of-factly. "A week is a long, long time, and I wanted to take him today."

"Oh brother," said Gia, rolling her eyes.

"But why did you run away?" asked Pippa.

"I heard Big Rob telling someone that Stroodle was too young to be away from Peaches, and I got scared. So I hid with Stroodle here."

Pippa shook her head.

"Well, you have a lot of people searching for you," she scolded. "Oh gosh! I still have to tell Mom and Britt we found you!"

Pippa sent a group text to include both of them and Pops:

Pippa: Found Ryan. Safe and sound. Stroodle 2 :)

"Ya know," Pippa said, turning back to Ryan, "you are lucky Stroodle remembered where you were. Gia found a piece of your t-shirt stuck to the fence, and then when we found Stroodle, I let him smell it ... and after one whiff of it, he showed us where you were! That's pretty amazing for a puppy!"

Ryan was distracted. Stroodle was slobbering all over his face.

"We're lucky you are so stinky!" laughed Gia.

Ryan made a pouty face and then started to laugh too. The four of them slowly made their way out of the pipe. Pippa held Ryan's hand, and Gia carried Stroodle. They carefully returned through the field so as not to get caught up in blackberry brush again.

In the distance, Britt heard them coming and made her way to the fence. One by one, she watched her friends crawl on all fours through the gap. When they stood up, she gave each of them a big hug. Ryan got an extra squeeze.

"Ryan. You gave us a big scare," she said, sighing heavily. "The whole camp is looking for you!"

"I'm just glad Stroodle could find you before dark and that you aren't hurt," added Pippa.

Pippa looked at Britt.

"Sorry we were away longer than twenty minutes. Are you okay, Britt?"

Britt nodded.

"I'm more than okay, now that you are all back safe and sound."

The Rescue

The rescue team joined the pooped-out pack as an orange sun set behind the hills. Big Rob lifted Ryan up.

"You feel like a sack of potatoes," he guffawed. "You wore yourself out."

Pippa held Stroodle close to her chest, and he chomped on her braids. Britt held onto her arm. Gia checked to see that none of Ryan's things were left behind, and they hiked back to camp. Several minutes later, Ryan was reunited with his parents.

"Mom, Pops," he said, surprised. "What are you doing here?"

"Oh Ryan," said Pippa. "Really?"

She gave Stroodle some nuzzles and offered him the piece of Ryan's Blue Frog Squad t-shirt, hoping he would surrender her braids. Stroodle wagged his tail and bit into the t-shirt enthusiastically.

"So it looks like you have another Ryan adventure to tell us, Pippa," Pops winked.

"Yup," answered Pippa. "And this one's a doozy!"

"A Labradoozy!" laughed Ryan, hugging Pippa and Stroodle together.

Chapter Nine

Just Jamie Jones

The next morning on Wigglers Island, Pippa, Britt, and Gia were playing with the puppies down at the lake. Everyone had finished breakfast, including the pups, and a little frolic before nap time was keeping them all busy. The water was calm, ideal for an early morning water ski. Not today, however. Today, the news station was sending over a reporter to interview the girls about yesterday's hunt for Ryan and Stroodle. The news about the adventure at Forest Wood Village Camp had spread fast. The reporter was due to arrive any moment.

The air felt cool against Pippa's face, and she zipped up her jacket to chase away the chill. Still, there was a blue sky overhead. Butterflies fluttered in her stomach. It felt more like wriggling worms. *It's probably just some nervous excitement before the interview*, she thought to herself. *I've never been on TV before.*

"Pippa!" Pops called out from the house. "The news crew is at the bridge."

"Okay, we will be right there!" Pippa called back. She turned to her friends. "Let's go, everyone, and see what this is all about."

They collected the pups and hurried up the hill to the house. Bilberry and Peaches followed along, circling each other and unaffected by the excitement. Two golf carts pulled up with three people and lots of equipment. A young woman popped out of the cart. Her long, brown-blonde hair was up in a ponytail, and she stood almost six feet tall.

"Hi, girls! I'm Jamie Jones," she announced brightly as if she were already on TV. "We are here to interview you about the incredible rescue yesterday. Are you ready to talk about your part in all of it?"

"Hi Jamie," Pippa boomed in a voice to match. "I'm Pippa Pinkerton, and these are my friends, Giovanna Lopez and Brittany Cline."

"Oh, you can call me Gia," said Gia.

"You can call me Britt," said Britt.

"And you can call *me* Pippa," giggled Pippa.

Britt and Gia started giggling too. Pippa's mom set down a playpen under the tree, and the girls helped put the pups inside as Jamie Jones addressed Pippa's parents.

"Mr. and Mrs. Pinkerton," said Jamie Jones, grinning and shaking both of their hands.

"You can call me Pops," said Pops, winking at Pippa.

"I'm noticing a trend," laughed Jamie.

"I'm Suzanne," Pippa's mom smiled. "We're so happy you're here!"

"Alrighty," said Jamie, getting down to business. She turned to the girls. "Which one of these is the famous pup who led you to the pipe?"

Pippa held up Stroodle.

"This is Stroodle, my Labradoodle," she said proudly to the reporter. "He led us right to my brother after smelling his stinky piece of camp t-shirt."

Pops chuckled. Jamie looked down at Stroodle.

"Wow," she said. "Stroodle the Labradoodle, huh? What determination!"

She scratched Stroodle behind the ears.

"Stroodle," she said to him, "you are so brave and *so* orange!"

Stroodle jumped up and licked Jamie Jones in the face. They all started laughing.

"Actually, his color is apricot," corrected Pippa. "He is the only one of his siblings with that color too."

"Interesting," said Jamie. "I imagine Stroodle will go to a very good home."

Pippa's heart skipped a beat. She suddenly felt irritated. *Doesn't Jamie Jones know that I am going to keep Stroodle? He's mine.*

"So," said Jamie loudly, bringing Pippa back to earth, "let's set up over here under the treehouse," she directed. "This looks like a nice spot to film."

Suddenly, high on top of the attic platform, Ryan streaked across the sky on the zipline and landed softly on the deck of the treehouse.

"I'm Ryanhood, the Prince of Trees!" he exclaimed. "Can I be on TV too, Miss Jones?"

Pippa shot a glance over at Pops.

"When did he have time to become Ryanhood?"

Jamie Jones laughed. Pops shrugged and threw up his hands.

"The adventures continue!"

"So you are the one," Jamie said, grinning playfully at Ryan. "Just Jamie is fine, Master Ryanhood."

"Okay, Just Jamie. Can I be on TV too?"

"Of course you can!" she replied brightly. "After all, you are the one Stroodle tracked to the pipe!"

"Yup. I am," said Ryan stoutly. "He is my best friend."

"And your hero," Jamie coached him. "Remember that when we start filming. Okay everyone, gather around."

Gia and Britt smoothed their blouses and shorts and then fixed each other's hair. Pippa held Stroodle. Earlier that morning, Mrs. Pinkerton had braided Pippa's hair into two long braids and wove little violets from the garden into them. Pippa wore a little lip gloss to match. Reddy, Ruby, Tippy, Polly, Lolly, and Ku'uipo were nestled down in their playpen while Peaches and Bilberry napped alongside.

The excitement mounted when Jamie's assistant instructed the girls to look into the camera and smile. They all squealed with anticipation, except Pippa. She tried to smile, but she was distracted. She kept replaying what Jamie had said earlier about Stroodle going to a good home. She shook her head. She was more determined than ever to have Stroodle become the newest addition to the *Pinkerton* home.

Gia snapped Pippa out of her thoughts.

"C'mon Pippa, pay attention."

Pippa looked over at the assistant who was writing on a small chalkboard with a hinge at the top. She took a deep breath in and put her Stroodle-free arm around Gia. Britt put her arm around Pippa. The three girls swayed left and right together.

"Everything will turn out okay, Pippa," said Britt, sensing her friend's anxiety.

"Thanks, Britt," said Pippa. "I appreciate you so much."

Pippa's parents looked on from a distance, watching the interview and keeping an eye on Ryan. The camerawoman called, "Rolling!" and the assistant held the chalkboard in front of the camera.

"Stroodle the Amazing Labradoodle," he said clearly. "Take one!"

He clapped the chalkboard pieces together and then walked out of the camera frame. Jamie Jones watched him as he counted down silently, using his fingers, "7, 6, 5, …" Pippa counted in her head down to one. At one, Jamie Jones started speaking.

"This is Jamie Jones, reporting to you from Wigglers Island in Frog Pond Lake. Just yesterday, five-year-old Ryan Pinkerton was reported missing from Forest Wood Village Camp. But don't worry, folks, this story has a happy ending. I will now introduce to you the three girls who found Ryan Pinkerton with the help of a two-month-old puppy, Stroodle the Labradoodle…"

Aside from Ryan running through the shots and requiring three different takes, everything went smoothly. The girls were excited to see the photos Mrs. Pinkerton took while they were filming.

"I already posted the good ones on our Frog Pond

Labradoodles website," Mrs. Pinkerton told them proudly. "I also posted a brief synopsis of the story. When the news report comes out, I'll include a link to it. I am excited to see how many people will be interested in our talented Doodle pup!"

"Everyone will see us on TV too!" Ryan cheered.

"Oh no!" cried Pippa. She turned to Gia and Britt. "Now everyone will want Stroodle for their own. What have I done?"

Chapter Ten

Stroodle's New Digs

That night, Pippa cried herself to sleep and woke abruptly from the same nightmare—Stroodle going to a new family and maybe never seeing him again. She stared up at the ceiling.

"Why why?" she howled frantically. She kicked off her bedsheets, got up, and started pacing her room. "I don't want to send Stroodle away! He's mine, mine, mine!"

She threw herself back onto her bed and started to cry. She sobbed so loudly and for so long, her face turned beet red, and her pillow was sopping wet with tears. She rolled over at the sound of her bedroom door opening. It was Ryan.

"Pippa, what's wrong?" asked Ryan. "Why is your face as red as a raspberry?"

Pippa gasped for air.

"Because I agreed to do the interview about Stroodle finding you in the pipe. And now everyone wants our Stroodle for their own." She sobbed harder. "The website showed interest from over fifty families, and that was only in one night. I am afraid to check it today. We won't be able to see him ever again."

Ryan wasn't sure what to do. He stared bewildered at his sister, who was overcome with grief. Just then, there was a knock on the door, and Mr. and Mrs. Pinkerton came into the room.

"Pippa, honey," comforted her mom, "what is it? What's the matter?"

"What's the *matter*?" roared Pippa through her tears. "How can you even ask that? I am never going to see Stroodle again."

"Pippa," said Pops gently. "Wait a minute..."

"Everyone wants him," Pippa interrupted.

"Pippa," insisted Pops. "Yes, we have had so many interested families in such a short amount of time, and we have come to a decision."

"What?" she blurted back. "Already? How can you make

your mind up so quickly with so many applicants? Don't you even care what I think?"

"Yes, of course we do," said Mrs. Pinkerton. "The decision was very easy. We all know this family quite well."

Pippa was bewildered. *What's happening? Who could this family be?*

Her mom continued, "Pops and I reviewed the list, and we both agreed that we found the best family to raise Stroodle. They have a great yard; they are really familiar with Labradoodles; and there are four people in the family to look after Stroodle. He won't get lonely."

Pippa was about to throw herself into her wet pillow again when Pops said, "Pippa! *We* are that family. It's us, the Pinkertons!"

"Whaat?" Pippa asked blearily.

"You heard me right," said Pops. "We are going to raise Stroodle. Your mom and I looked at your list of reasons to keep him, and we agreed on every single one of them. We will let you decide which skills Stroodle should learn first so that he can become a comfort dog or an assistant to your mom, whatever you think. You can take the lead on seeing where Stroodle's strong points are and then go with it. You are in charge."

"Um," said Ryan, "just don't choose the 'Keep-Ryan-out-of-trouble' one."

Pops and Mrs. Pinkerton chuckled. Pippa smiled weakly.

"Just wait and see," Ryan continued, "Stroodle is going to be my partner in crime. He can be my Little John!"

Pippa began to cry again.

"What is wrong now?" Ryan asked, confused. "Don't you understand? We get to keep Stroodle!"

"I'm crying because I'm so relieved and shocked and happy," Pippa said.

She sat up and took a couple of deep breaths in and out. She looked at her mom.

"I will teach Stroodle and practice with him every day. Thanks, Mom and Pops. I love you like crazy!"

Ryan climbed onto Pippa's bed and jumped up and down.

"Okay everyone, time to eat breakfast! I'm *hungry* like crazy!" Everyone laughed. Pippa gave each of her parents and Ryan a big hug, and together they trampled down the stairs for some good old-fashioned peanut butter French toast.

After breakfast, Pippa looked in on Stroodle and the few pups who remained, waiting for their new owners to bring them home. She lay down on the floor, smiling as they frolicked around her.

"Stroodle!" she gushed at her new puppy. "We did it! You

are staying right here where you belong. I have to text my besties, but I wanted *you* to know first."

Stroodle looked at Pippa as if to say, *Of course I'm staying here. I am at home with you.* Pippa's heart was full. She was happier than she had been in a long time. She picked up Stroodle and nuzzled his furry orange face.

ACKNOWLEDGMENTS

I am blessed to have my accomplished children involved in this process of writing and publishing. Jamie Lynn, your encouragement, guidance, and skills are exemplary. Erik, I could not have published this without you – your support and technological strength are invaluable. Ryan, there could be no Stroodle if it wasn't for your antics and your uncanny ability to find yourself in comical situations. Zuzana, your positivity and tenacity are truly motivating. Megan, your love of books inspired me to further explore my writing capabilities with confidence and to always remember to have fun with it. Jason, your service to this nation reminds me to seize the American Dream every day; thanks to you and to Jamie Lynn for your incomparable service to our country.

I'd like to extend a heartfelt thanks to my teammates who supported me through this project from start to finish. Paulina Jaeger, my editor and writing coach. What a gift! To the illustrator, Heidi Jay, you make the story come alive with your imagination and talent. To Jeanne Provost, my life coach, yoga guru, and spirit guide – namaste. Amanda Miller, my Publishing Consultant, who is fabulous at the finish line! Susi Jawurek for your help handling the business management. Deni Casteel, thanks for all the walks and talks at our hilltop office where you provided input on Stroodle!

I'm also grateful for my BESTIES, my mentors, and my family and friends – both new and old – in Belgium, Slovakia, and in the USA. I appreciate every one of you for your optimism and true friendship. Also, to my parents, Jeannie, Roz, and Amalda. And finally, saving the best for last, my man MARC! Married to me for over forty years! Dedicated! Love you always! Thank you to the Finke Labradoodle, my model. Ruff Ruff.

ABOUT THE AUTHOR

Teri's true love is entertaining kids. Her favorite moments are spent with her four grandchildren playing games, throwing tea parties, singing chants, and climbing trees. Stroodle's adventures started when Teri discovered her love of storytelling as a teen, writing about her doodle pup, Coco La Moco, and her Cat, Karate. She kept a journal for many years recording her comical life experiences so she could write more about them later. She has also written many articles for the medical field, charities, and church, and even wrote a monthly family blog before blogs were popular.

Teri lives in the Pacific Northwest in a small Kentucky farmhouse, where she and her husband have managed twelve horses, raised three kids, and loved four dogs over the past 25 years. Her evenings are spent gazing at the incredible sunsets from her deck and imagining new stories for her readers about Stroodle the Labradoodle.

ABOUT THE ILLUSTRATOR

Heidi has been drawing ever since she was old enough to hold a pencil and pencil sketches are still one of her most favorite things to do. This is her third collaboration with TLS DeCoster. The first collaboration was an alphabet coloring book, in which Pippa was first introduced for the delightful character that she is. Besides illustrating children's books, Heidi knits, paints murals, has designed graphic art for country music bands, created graphic work for gamers and designed art exhibits and merchandise. When she isn't working on an art project, Heidi can be found at the barn, teaching students and riding horses. A horse trainer for many years, she also works with non-profits, high school riding teams and horse clubs to promote good handling and horsemanship. Heidi rides, paints and illustrates in the Pacific Northwest. She loves the rain!

STROODLETHELABRADOODLE.COM